The Story William Jex

A 22-year-old nineteenth century Mormon convert emigrates from Norfolk, England, to seek The Promised Land in America. A compelling account of extreme danger, privations, polygamy and founding a dynasty.

Nick Turner

The Story of
William Jex

Nick Turner

Designed by Reflex Graphic Design - 01225 832551

ISBN 9781916102897 Published by Barton Muse Publishing, 1 Soutergate, Barton upon Humber, DN18 5HG

Foreword

My maternal grandfather, Albert Edward Jex, was born in Gorleston, Norfolk in 1884. His unusual surname made working on his family tree fairly easy and going back a few years I discovered the man who inspired me to write this tribute: he was William Jex, born in Crostwick, Norfolk in 1831. At first, I thought that he would be an unremarkable figure, but I soon discovered that there was nothing ordinary about William and my five-year search into his story began.

The family of William Jex. Photograph taken on William's 94th birthday, September 5th 1925, Spanish Fork, Utah. William is seated, centre front.

Here's how it started. On March 10th, 1853 William heard a Mormon missionary speaking in the Market Place in Norwich about a new religion, and his life changed totally and for ever. He became a member of the Mormon Church, emigrated to America and made his way by steam-boat up the Mississippi and wagon train across the Great Plains to the Utah territory, where Mormons were building their new community in the wilderness: Deseret, they called it.

The difficulties which William faced in reaching Deseret were little short of monumental; cholera, small pox, starvation, the vast distances, hostile Native Americans and violence were ever present.

But William never gave up: whatever challenges appeared he overcame them. He never complained: his unshakable faith sustained him.

I am not a Mormon, but the more I learned about William the more my respect for him grew and he has a very special place in my family tree.

— ooOOoo —

William lived at a time when African Americans and Native Americans were referred to in terms that are unacceptable today, but I have used the terms where I quote William's spoken and written words to maintain authenticity. I apologise if, in doing this, I have caused offence. Similarly, I have referred to practices and opinions emanating from the Mormon Church and its followers in William's time which are no longer relevant. Again, I have tried to be historically accurate and no offence is intended.

Finally, I would like to thank Monty Martin and the other members of Barton upon Humber's Mill Writers' Group for their invaluable help and advice.

Chapter 1

September 5th 1925, Spanish Fork, Utah

William Jex

Today is my 94th birthday. 94! The Lord has been truly good to me to preserve me so long. I've a few aches, but nothing to complain about, 'cept having to get up in the night to do a you know what. Could be a lot worse, I guess. Folks have been coming for days now from all over to celebrate, mostly from here, Spanish Fork, and Salt Lake City, but as well from places out of State. ''Going to have you a party,'' they say. "Have a bath, Grandpa,'' they say. "Put your suit on.'' "Brush your hair''. "Clean your shoes.'' "Where's your teeth?

'Why?' I say.

'Cause it's your birthday. 94! All the family are coming and you're having a party,'' granddaughter Sarah says. "And you're not to do no cussing! You're supposed to be an Elder,''.

'Last time I counted there was over 200 of 'em. Who's paying? And I'll do as much cussing as I like!'

'Now Grandpa! Don't be like that. It's a big thing, 94 years old and still going strong. You'll enjoy a party and there's a photographer coming all the way from Salt Lake City. He wants to put your picture in the paper and you might even get something written about you. How about that? 'William Jex, Pioneer and Patriarch'. Doesn't that sound grand? Wouldn't that be great? One of us, right there in the newspaper for everybody to see. So don't forget to put a clean collar on, and wear a tie.'

I told her that it all sounded like vanity, something I've opposed all my life because it's against the Church's teaching, but I suppose this won't do much harm at my time of life. Come to think of it perhaps it would be good to have something written about what I've done in my 94 tears. Couldn't do it myself, though: I'm no scholar. I'll have to get one of the young 'uns to write down what I say and set it out all clever – proper spelling an' all. Come to think about it, it'd take more than a few lines in a newspaper to tell my story: more like a whole goddam' book. Sarah might help with it: she's smart and needs something to occupy herself. She's had it tough: tougher than most. First, she lost her husband, – heart attack, took him quick. And then she lost one of her boys in France seven years ago. He was in a machine gun detachment of the U.S. third Division at a place called Chateau Thierry. I wish he'd never have volunteered. We should keep out of European wars. The Elders say that the War was God's punishment of sinful governments and I 'd go along with that. But you can't put an old head on young shoulders and the poor boy died.

The more I think about it, the more I like the idea of telling my story. Of course, I'd want to make it plain that I owe everything to the Church, - the Church of Jesus Christ of Latter-Day Saints as some call it; or just the Mormons, or Saints. Everything I've done as a grown man has been guided by my faith; every business deal, every decision, every breath I've taken. And I've needed plenty of guidance in my 94 years; leaving my old life back in England and cutting myself off from family and friends for ever (as I thought at the time); crossing the ocean and travelling to the farthest limits of the new world, Deseret, as we called it then; the Mississippi, Indians, the endless prairie. But you know what I remember most about the journey here? It was the comradeship: the people who shared their dreams and struggled together to face up to every challenge we came across, sharing everything and building friendships that would last to the ends of our lives. The memories come flooding back to me now as fast as I can think. Yes, it would be good to remember those days.

There were good times and bad. And plenty of hard work. Young folk now don't realise what we did in those early years, forcing a living out of the bare earth with tools we made ourselves; working all the hours God sent. And helping each other 'cause as sure as Hell nobody else would. We even took on the US Army one time when the Government tried to interfere; formed our own Militia and all.

We lived our lives then in the blinding light of our faith, knowing that the Lord was guiding us. But I'm getting ahead of myself here. I can see through the window all the folks getting ready to have the family photograph taken. That feller there must be the photographer from Salt Lake City, taking his gear out of that shiny new automobile. Better move myself quick. Don't want Sarah getting sore with me; she don't know it, but she's going to help me write this story. Now where's she put my clean collars?

Chapter 2

November 5th 1925, Spanish Fork, Utah

Well, I'm glad the party's over. It was about a couple of months ago and it all went well. It was good to see my family, even though – and don't spread this around – I didn't recognise most of the young 'uns. And I got tired with all the fussing about. The best part for me was the singing. Our Tabernacle choir sang my favourite hymn, "Shall We Gather at the River?' It was beautiful; it always brings tears to my old eyes.

But enough of that. You want to know about my story. Well, Sarah agreed to do the smartening up of what I say – providing I don't do too much cussing. I bought her one of those new typewriting machines out of the Sears and Roebuck catalogue. You should've seen her face when it arrived! She was like a kid with the best birthday present ever. OK then. Let's get started.

March 10, 1853 was the day that changed my life. Or I should say that it was the day when my new life truly began. I can remember it as clear as day; but I couldn't tell you what I did yesterday! Now, I'm getting you confused and I haven't gotten started. Let me say it clear: that was the day I decided that that I would be a follower of Mormon. I hadn't intended to make such an important decision at that time, although I had been thinking about it for a month or two, but when I saw that evil man, dressed like a preacher and mocking good people I realised that what I was witnessing that day was the difference between right and wrong as clear as day and I knew that I had to choose which side I was on.

I'd better explain. I remember that it was a fine early spring morning. I was with my brothers, mother, sister, sister-in-law and my closest friend, Horace Howlett. Horace was my employer's son and I was First Man on his farm. We had joined a large crowd of folks in the Market Place in Norwich, England, so that we could hear the speaker, John Johnson. He turned out to be a Mormon missionary. Well, he told us about the truly wonderful new religion that had started in America and was now spreading all over Europe. We knew a little about his message already and were eager to hear more. He was a good speaker and he soon had the crowd listening intently as he spoke of the Promised Land waiting for God's chosen people to gather together and settle there in a place called Deseret in the far west of America. He showed us maps of the new country in America – Deseret he called it, and another showing the almost identical valley of the river Jordan in the Holy Land. He explained how Jesus, after His Resurrection, had visited America and spoken with the Indians; how a man called Mormon had received the word of God written on sheets of solid gold.

It was wonderful and we were all listening, and some were crying and clapping. I realised that he was speaking about a real place, where true believers could build their own clean, new world and live their lives governed by their own church. It was like a thunderbolt hitting me. And I knew from that moment that the Lord had called me to join this new Church. I wept with joy.

And then we heard the drum. Heads turned at the sound and I saw a poorly dressed man banging a drum and leading a parade of strange looking folks. The drummer was a short, fat man wearing a priest's cassock. He was unsteady on his feet and clearly drunk. Behind him was another drunkard wearing an old jacket, ragged corduroy trousers and muddy boots, and I was puzzled at first to see a card bearing the word 'Groom' pinned to his chest. Walking close to him were three common looking women dressed like brides, but very ragged if you know what I mean. They had painted faces and wore flowering weeds in their hair. They held bouquets of cow parsley and dandelions and were shouting and jeering at speaker, Johnson. Fixed to their clothing, they had cards bearing the inscription 'Bride 1', 'Bride 2,' and 'Bride 3'. With a shock of revulsion, I realised that these disgusting creatures were making a mockery of the Mormon wedding ceremony. It had just about then become the practice for some Mormon men to take more than one wife – some of them little more than children - and it had caused a lot of trouble for us back then in England as well as here in America. Still does. I'll talk more about that later.

'Hurry up and get on with it, Parson!' shouted one of the three trollops (for they truly deserved the title). 'It's nearly my bed time.'

'Clock hasn't stopped you afore, Charlotte,' shrieked one of the other women, causing the group to howl with laughter. And I noticed that some of the crowd joined in and I realised that a good few were there to cause trouble.

The wretched group stood in front of the speaker, Johnson, and began to go through the beautiful words of the marriage service that we all knew; but this time the false preacher made them dirty with his crude twisting of the message and the filthy gestures which he shamelessly made in front of respectable folk. He put down his drum, took a black book from his pocket, looked at the 'groom' and asked, nodding towards the three trollops and slapping the backside of each one in turn with his book, "Do you take this woman, and this 'n and this 'n to be -----"-) The rest was drowned out by raucous laughter And there was more obscene ridicule when the false preacher asked the crowd if anyone present knew of any impediment to the marriage to speak up or forever hold his peace.

The meeting then fell apart, with crude gestures, shouting and pushing; a few stones were thrown. If the women had not been with me, I believe that I would have struck down the false preacher, his ugly sneering face laughing at the way he had tried to destroy a moment of beautiful revelation, but I couldn't risk exposing them to the growing violence and I told our party to get away fast.

In the following few weeks Horace and I and a few others spoke often about that incident and became more angry at what had happened. And you know what, more things like that were happening all the time; Mormon meetings were being broken up by drunken mobs and the official Church did nothing to stop them – Priests even whipped up hatred of us in their sermons. People got hurt and were often chased through the streets by folks who had once been their friends and neighbours. It was happening all over the country; Mormon property was set on fire and I heard of one place where a Mormon was forced to fire a shotgun over the heads of a mob in order to save his family. I began to feel that I no longer belonged in my own country and that people I had known all my life had turned against me.

We often thought that we'd just have to take this foulness on the chin, but I couldn't get the sight of that drummer out of my mind and I was all for striking back hard – why should those foul mouthed, ignorant bastards control us. We were honest hard-working people who just wanted to live our lives in peace. Why couldn't they leave us alone? Folks don't realise that I could have been a violent man. Yes, me! You all see me as a Patriarch of the Church who has dedicated his life to the Holiness of the Lord. But as a young and ignorant man I'm ashamed to say that I could use my fists and I remember at that time being sorely tempted.

Anyway, I remember that Horace and me, we often talked about what the Mormon preacher had told us. A few others were as interested as we were and we joined together whenever we could to talk about the new faith and the wonderful land of Deseret. But as the actions against us grew worse I became very low in spirits: all I could do was to pray for a solution to our problem, though, to be honest, I didn't think it would do any good. Me and Horace, we decided that the only answer was for us to follow the urging of the Church and take part in what we called 'the Gathering': we should leave England and go to America, to help build, with other Mormons, our new faith and community and leave all that misery and hatred behind.

But there was a bug in the ointment – we had no money. As First Man on Howlett's farm my wages were 25 shillings a week. Can't work out what that'd be in our money now, but I can tell you that it wasn't much! How could we find enough money to let us live our dream?

Whenever Mormons have a problem, we ask the Lord for help. And that's just what me and Horace did. The Lord listened and helped us: He put an idea into the head of Horace's Pa and made him make a plan. The old man didn't like the Mormons so he told Horace that he could either abandon those "wicked Mormons", as he called us, and eventually have a share of the family farm in his will, or he could have forty pounds right away and go to America and stay there! Well, that got things moving: the old man thought that Horace would back down, but did he Hell! He accepted the money and left his Pa fuming.

Pretty soon a group of us got together and raised more money. We sold everything we owned and borrowed some from the Church, promising to pay it back in cash or labour as soon as we could. Speaker John Johnson helped us make the arrangements. We were to go to a place called Great Yarmouth, that's on the East coast of England, and go by sea to Liverpool. From there we would cross the ocean to New Orleans. Then, Johnson said, we would go up the Mississippi to Kansas and then go by wagon for a thousand miles west to our new country and our new lives. Our party was to consist of myself, Horace Howlett, John Lambert and his wife, my deceased brother Richard's widow (Eliza), and their young daughter. Later a few other friends joined us. Our departure date was set for February 8, 1854. John Johnson made all the arrangements for us; he was a very smart man.

But what Johnson could not do was to tell me how to leave my mother. That was a painful thing, and I don't want to talk about it right now. Maybe later.

Chapter 3

November 12th 1925, Spanish Fork, Utah

I'm getting to like these trips down Memory Lane with Sarah. She brings me cookies and I make coffee and I remember things from so long ago. Other folks have found out about this writing of ours and have gotten curious about what I'm saying, but they'll just have to wait. Sometime I'm going to tell about things that are a little embarrassing: I haven't always been a Patriarch! Like what I'm going to reveal today, I guess.

It's about my first wife, Eliza. Well, she was strictly speaking my sister-in-law at first, married to my brother, Richard. I'd taken a fancy to her then, but Richard had gotten there first. Anyway, Richard died and went to Glory, leaving behind Eliza and their little girl. I tried to comfort her like a brother, but we soon realised that we wanted more than a brother – sister relationship. We went to the vicar of the church in Crostwick, where I was born; this was well before we became Mormons you understand, and said that we wanted to marry. But that old vicar, he said we couldn't marry

Eliza Goodson Jex in later life

as we were related; brother and sister-in-law. I tried to get round that by saying that we weren't blood related, but he wouldn't budge. Said it would be something called 'a marriage of affinity' and it would be illegal. It had always been illegal for hundreds of years. Stupid business.

But it was true. Eliza and I loved each other, but we couldn't be together. We just had to be careful, especially when we both became Mormons. We managed to keep our love under wraps, hoping that somehow in time we could live openly as man and wife. And then the Lord was good to us. He gave us the courage to marry without the old church and its crazy old laws. We weren't going to let an outdated piece of paper get in the way of our happiness. So, we went ahead anyway and this is how we did it: our party left Crostwick and travelled to Liverpool on the first bit of our journey to America, we had a few days to wait there until our ship docked. So, Eliza and I asked Mormon Elder Daniel Karns to marry us, which he did on February 22, 1854. We were both twenty-eight years old and little Sarah was just three. And that was how our new lives together began.

Sarah Anne (left) was born in 1851 in Crostwick, Norfolk, the daughter of Eliza Goodson/Jex who married William Jex's brother. After the brother died, Eliza married William Jex on 22nd February 1854 and travelled with them, known as Sarah Anne Jex as they sailed from Liverpool to America the same day. When she was seventeen years-old she married Joshua Brockbank becoming Sarah Anne Brockbank and had thirteen children. She died, aged seventy-seven in 1928 in Spanish Fork, Utah.

We were married in the morning and later the same day me and Eliza and the rest of our party went on board the 'Windermere'. There were lots of other Mormons on board as the ship had been chartered by our Church and we were all on our way to the Promised Land. We sang happy hymns of praise as a steam tug towed our ship out of the docks and into open water. But we soon stopped singing as we met the heaving ocean and sea sickness began. Our accommodation was very rough; with bunk beds, old dirty blankets and no privacy. There wasn't even a seat of ease; only buckets! 477 Mormons were packed into the hold of the ship and we were far from being happy, but our troubles were only just beginning.

The ship had a medical officer - don't think he was a proper doc. He gave everybody an examination and even though half of us were so seasick we could hardly stand he said we were all fine. But I knew different – I didn't feel well at all and after a few days of fever I got a rash and then raised spots filled with fluid and knew I'd gotten the small pox. I reckon the old dirty blankets were to blame. Soon, other folks got the same disease. The weather was so rough the captain said we were all to stay below so we had no fresh air, and hardly any light. Those days were like Hell; about half the people had the small pox; most were sea sick; the buckets were full to overflowing and the weather worsened. There was nothing we could do but sit or lie there in that filthy mess, in the dark mostly and listening to the tempest and the cries of women and children.

We were at the mercy of westerly gales that lasted for nearly two months and made our progress very slow. Some days the winds were so strong we were forced to run with them and we lost a lot of progress. And the Windermere wasn't all that safe: water was spurting through the planked sides and the captain had to have men pumping for hours on end. They didn't like that especially as the ship was short of crewmen. The Windermere was one of the last wooden sailing ships to carry passengers across the Atlantic and remember, it was winter – the worst time of year to make the crossing – and some of the crew had refused to make the voyage and had stayed behind in Liverpool waiting for better weather and a safer ship.

Well, the small pox ran its course – the medical officer was no use, drunk most of the time - and we lost eleven passengers to the disease. Their bodies were wrapped in canvas, weighted with lumps of coal from the galley and buried at sea by the crew: it was too rough for any of us to be allowed on deck to attend the funerals of our friends: the waves were now breaking clear over the ship and even Captain Fairfield began to fear that the ship would break up and we would all be lost. He came below to speak to us and told us to prepare for the worst. Our Elders said that we would pray for deliverance. ''You pray; I'll pump,'' said the captain.

Well, the Lord heard our prayers because the tempest died down overnight. Next morning, we were allowed up on deck to find the sun shining in a cloudless sky, a fresh easterly breeze and the 'Windermere' sailing faster than we had seen before. The women folk asked the captain to let them have some fresh water to wash their small clothes, as salt made them kind of rough and scratchy. But the captain said that we were too short of fresh water and it could only be used for drinking. The weather stayed like fine and we made the last 1000 miles of our voyage in just over 7 days. We dropped anchor just

Steamboat landing, New Orleans

off New Orleans and gave heartfelt thanks for our deliverance.

We were not allowed to land because we'd had cases of small pox and were quarantined for two weeks before we could go ashore. Some of our group were so weakened by the ordeal of our voyage from Liverpool that our Elders made arrangements for them to stay in hospital in New Orleans until they had recovered their strength and could follow the rest of us. We didn't have much time to spare – only a few days, and spent the time in pretty rough lodging houses that the local Mormon agent had fixed up for us. At first, we found that the solid ground was so strange to us after the motion of the ship that we staggered about as if we were in liquor! The place made quite an impact on all of us; first we couldn't hardly understand anybody: they all seemed to speak either French or very strange English. But the sight that shocked us most was seeing black people – men, women and children, most of them stark naked, – being sold in the streets, prodded and pushed about like cattle. Now, I know that our religion tells us that the black man is the servant of the white man, but I've got to say that the sight of human beings being treated like that did not sit easy with me. No Sir!

The next part of our journey was on board a big steam-powered stern paddle wheeler sailing north for about 1200 miles along the Mississippi/Missouri rivers to a place called Atcheson in Kansas. Railroads were few and far between, in those days – I'm talking 70 years ago, and remember, the Atlantic to Pacific track was just a dream then.

Sarah's getting a little upset by what I've been telling her: young 'uns don't realise how bad things were for us, the first groups of pioneers and think that it was all sitting in a wagon, crossing the continent in warm sunny weather and singing hymns all the time. Well, it wasn't nothing like that. It was a great disappointment to all of us when we set off from New Orleans on that big stern wheeler; there'd be no storms; no sea sickness and no small pox. No Sir; there was something much worse; something that struck terror into us in our exhausted, weakened state.

Soon after we'd left New Orleans one of the families on board, with the name of Snobell or Schnobl, something like that, well one morning they all began to feel ill. There was father, mother and four children. They were struck down with terrible diarrhoea and vomiting. And great pain in the belly. We asked for the captain to come and see them, which he did, pretty quick. He took one look at the unfortunate wretches and called for Sam, a black man who was   our pilot on that particular stretch of the river. Sam came into the cabin, he was an old, stooped man who seemed to be well regarded by most of the rest of the crew, in spite of his colour. The captain indicated the stricken family's necessary bucket with his boot and asked,

'What do you think of that, Sam?'

Sam picked up the bucket and moved towards the open door to get more light. He swilled the bucket round and then put his nose closer to it. He put the bucket down and raised his eyes to the captain.

'Rice water stool, Cap'n Sir?'

'You sure of that, Sam?'

'Sure, I'm sure, Cap'n, Sir. Seen it often enough. And it smells fishy. Always a dead giveaway.'

The captain nodded thoughtfully.

'Empty that bucket over the side and get back to the wheel house, there's shoal water round the net bend.'

'Yessir,' said Sam, and hurried off to obey the order.

The captain turned to face the anxious passengers. ''You know what rice water stool is?'' he asked, but his question was met with puzzled expressions.

'Well, you folks from Europe calls it cholera.' He paused to let his words sink in. 'But we got our own name for it here. That mess in the bucket looked like the water that's drained off after rice has been boiled. And it smells of fish. It's cholera'

The crowd of men and women were shocked but their stifled cries of horror and fear were stilled as the captain took control. He called for the men nearest him and took them to one side. He spoke quiet.

'They'll probably die pretty soon. And I guess there 'll be others; it spreads quick.'

Elder Karns asked what could be done and could they turn round and get medical help back in New Orleans

'I'll not take a boat full of cholera back into the city. Too risky. No, we'll carry on. All you can do for these folks and any other victims is give them clean water to drink: they'll be terrible thirsty. And try to keep everybody and the cabins clean'

By nightfall both Snobell parents and their oldest child, a girl, were dead and more folks had become ill. We were not allowed to bury our friends in the water, as we had done crossing the ocean. The captain explained that corpses drifting down the river could spread infection, so I and two other men rowed our departed brother and sisters to the shore where we managed to dig holes in the muddy soil, although the tangled tree roots made it difficult. The cholera took forty-two more of our party before it had run its course. We thanked the Lord that he had spared us.

Chapter 4

December 5th 1925, Spanish Fork, Utah

Heavy snowfall last night and bitterly cold this morning. I've been looking out of the window onto the street for half an hour or more. Ah! There she is! I can see Sarah now coming up through the snow to the front porch. Looks like she's gotten something interesting in that basket. Hope it's apple pie. Sarah sure makes a mean apple pie. I'll go let her in.

I thanked Sarah for the apple pie after I'd eaten a good slice and she left the rest of it on the side table for me to have later. Sarah just smiles and says that I deserve a little pampering, considering all that I've done for the people. I don't argue with her, besides, what little I've done has been what the Lord has told me to do. And I've been able to do it only because He gave me the strength to do it. Anyway, enough of that; let's get on with the story. Sarah's settled by the fire and has her notebook and pencil ready. She'll type it up neat and proper later.

Our party had reached Atchson, Kansas after several cruel months of travelling across the ocean and up the Mississippi/Missouri. Atcheson was the farthest west we could travel by water in a vessel of any size. From there we would have to walk a thousand miles to reach Deseret, the land of Zion, Utah, call it what you like.

Sarah looks at me with a frown. ''Walk?'' she asks.

'Walk, I repeated; only the sick rode in the heavily laden wagons.'

Atcheson was one of a few townships on the Kansas side of the river that were the starting points for many wagon trains heading west. It was a busy place; with saw mills, blacksmiths, stores warehouses, tanneries, gunsmiths, bakeries

Kansas Pioneers, a mid-19th Century painting by George Melville Stone.

and everywhere, cattle. And the noise they made! I'd never seen so many, and they all had to be broken in to haul the wagons. Our party was taken to the edge of town, divided into groups of 12 or15 or so and given a tent that would be our home on the trail from then until we would reach the Great Salt Lake in Utah.

From our first day in Atcheson everyone was put to work, doing whatever jobs were given to us. I said that I'd had some knowledge of timber and carpentry back in England so I found myself working in the wagon construction yard. The great Conestoga wagons were much larger than those I'd known in England: with neck yoke attached they were 24 feet long, 4 feet wide with an overall wheelbase of five feet and needed three pair of oxen to pull them. When I reported to the foreman in charge of wagon building, he smiled, pointed to a wagon that was almost finished and gave me a bucket of tar and a brush. Just because I was priest didn't stop me working with my hands; there were no free loaders in those days. I didn't expect any special treatment, and I sure wasn't given any.

'Get yourself under that wagon son,' the foreman said, 'and get a thick coat of tar on the underside. I don't want to see no gaps, just a thick coat of black.'

I took the bucket and brush and crawled under the huge Conestoga and realised that the only way I could do the job would be to lie on my left side and with my right-hand dip the brush into the bucket and reach up to work on the underside of the wagon. I soon began to feel the strain in my shoulder and then the tar trickled down the handle of the brush and soon my right side had a coat of tar. It was a long job, especially as the wagon wasn't flat. It had a kind of belly where barrels could be stored so that they wouldn't roll about on inclines. At last, it was finished and I crawled out of the confined space and saw the foreman looking at me and smiling.

'How many coats you put on, son?' he asked.

'You want me to put on another?'

'Sure I do, son. And try to get more on the wagon and less on yourself.'

But I enjoyed the work after the idleness of the last few months. The foreman didn't keep me 'on the tar' as he put it for long and put me on a construction gang when he saw that I knew my way around woodworking tools. I soon began to see an interesting possibility, which I kept to myself at the time: the timber was so good! And plentiful: there for the taking. Wonderful timber. Only trouble was cutting the trunks into the thicknesses that the Conestoga wagon builders needed. Black men were employed working in the saw pits but could only produce a limited amount each day and the sluggish river at that point didn't give enough fall to make water powered mills possible. So I thought to myself, 'Now think on this, Billy Boy, how about hitching up a saw mill onto a steam engine, like the one in that stern wheeler that brought us here?' And that's where the Jex Lumber Company began, but only in my head at that time.

It was there in the wagon building yard that I met one the most influential men I've ever known. I'd lost my Pa when I was eight years old, so I guess he became a sort of father to me. His name was William Phelps. He was sixty-two years old when I met him and was to be the leader of our wagon train; a God-fearing firebrand of a man and as tough as they make them. He'd been driven out first from Illinois and then Missouri with hundreds of other Mormons, at gun point, after they'd been forced to give up their homes, farms, possessions, weapons; everything, by the State governor, Lilburn Briggs. Their leaders were imprisoned without trial. Anyone who objected was to be exterminated, as the Governor's written order put it, by the State Militia. Briggs also ordered the execution, again without trial, of the Mormon leader, Joseph Smith. But the militia commander refused to carry out the order and Smith was quietly allowed to escape.

Phelps was bitterly angry about the way that the Mormons had been treated. Never seen a man so riled and I was shocked when I understood that he and the other older men were fully prepared to take military action to resist any attempts to drive them out of Utah. Phelps used to say, 'They drove us here but as sure as Hell, they ain't going to drive us out of Utah: there's no place else to go!' Mormons had set up a sizeable Militia force in Utah at that time and I eventually joined it when our homes were threatened. But that's another story; don't want to get ahead of myself.

Sarah's looking at me wide eyed and she's obviously shocked, just as I was when Phelps told me about it. But there's a lot more violence that I'll come to later.

Phelps spent time with me. At first, I found it difficult to open up to him as I had always had to be the tough man, leading others in our group, making decisions for them. But the journey so far had exhausted me as much as the others. I began to feel guilty that I had left my mother back in England to a life without a man or sons to help her. I spoke to Phelps about this. He listened: he was a good listener. He always used to say that the Lord had given men one mouth and two ears for a good reason. Trouble was, most damn fools got that the wrong way round. Well, he let me say all I wanted and then he asked me to look back on the journey so far; about crossing the ocean; the horrors of the disease on the Mississippi and about the most difficult part yet to come: the months of travel on foot, across the prairie. And then he asked me if my mother would have able to make such a trip; and I knew he was making me answer my own question: she wouldn't have made it.

The wagons were carefully loaded with everything we would need for the journey that would take about two months. We had to travel clear across Kansas and Nevada in the summer to be sure of finding forage and water for the oxen. Horses and mules are pretty useless for hauling heavy wagons: they come to a block of some kind; a rock, a gopher hole, patch of swamp, anything like that and the wagon stops dead. You crack your whip; the horses jerk sudden like and sure as God made little green apples, they break the traces. But oxen, why they just lean into the harness, real slow and heave the wagon away safe. Give me oxen every time.

The Mormon agents in Atcheson had insisted that each group of emigrants had to include at least fifty armed men and enough horses to have a screen of mounted guards riding at distance from the wagons at all times. We were supplied with food, tools, clothing, ammunition and seeds: everything we would need to reach Utah and then get started on our new lives. My wagon had a milk cow tied to the tail board because we had some little 'uns. All the wagons carried a bucket of axle grease gainhand to stop the screeching of raw wood as all those wagons started to move.

We soon settled down into a routine as we pushed westward. We were a pretty mixed bunch; mostly English, but there were a couple of family groups from Iceland and some refugees from the anti-Mormon mobs in Illinois and Mississippi. We travelled between ten to fifteen miles a day, according to the land and stopped when we found grazing and water. A bugle call told the drivers to circle the wagons and corral the animals; tents were erected and guards sent out. Children were sent off to collect kindling and buffalo chips for the cooking fires. Another bugle call ordered fires lit and food prepared, latrine pits dug and screened. After supper the people were called to prayer and finally a last call had all fires and lights put out and the folks went to their beds. Only the slowly circling mounted guards, changed at midnight, stayed awake. There were wolves about, but they were too wary of such a large train to come close.

Just before dawn more bugle calls roused the people from their beds for morning prayers. Food was prepared, porridge or the like; animals rounded up, tents struck and the train set off on another day's journey. Day after day, week after week we pushed on across the sea of grass under the clear blue sky, towards a horizon that never changed. We then realised what it meant to be alone: so far on our journey from England we had been helped by ships' captains and Church agents, but now we had to rely on ourselves: there was no one else.

We saw lots of buffalo. And once had to stop because a herd of hundreds blocked our way and held us up for a whole day. We didn't try to shoot any as the gunshot might have spooked them and started a stampede, although I've eaten buffalo meat since then and it's real tasty. Bit strong, but tasty.

We came across a few bands of Indians. They came to us careful at first until they found we were Mormons and then became friendly. Our Church teaches us that the Indians were descended from one of the twelve lost tribes of Israel and that Jesus himself had visited America after his resurrection and had spoken to them, so we were always kind to them and even gave them small presents. We had to go easy on that after a while because some of them started asking us for guns and ammunition which we would not do and they became surly when we refused and acted like spoiled children. Dangerous spoiled children; more about that later!

After about a month, one of the wheels on the lead wagon began to give us concern. The dry, hot weather had shrunk the wooden rim and expanded the iron tire. If the tire came off the wheel would break. We tried to cure the problem by driving the wagon into a stream and leaving it there overnight to soak and swell the wooden wheel. This worked for a while but one afternoon the tire did come off; the wheel just fell apart and the wagon fell sideways, crushing the leg of a woman walking alongside. Her screams alerted the whole train and everything stopped.

The woman's husband, one of the Icelanders in the party, gave orders to the gathering crowd and sent men to a nearby copse to cut a length of timber long enough to make a lever. Other folks were set to emptying the wagon and children were kept away from the screaming woman. Well, that lever worked and the wagon was lifted by a dozen men hauling on it. The poor woman was gently pulled from underneath the wagon so we could see what her injuries were. Her thigh bone was broken, but the bone had not broken through the skin. We knew that there was a risk that an artery could have been damaged and she might die from internal bleeding. But that was a risk we had to take. The woman was held down by the others in her tent group and her leg was firmly set straight and tightly secured by hastily made wooden splints. She had fainted by this time and the treatment was done firmly. She was placed gently into the second wagon, a spare wheel put onto the raised wagon and as soon as the loads were replaced, we continued on our way.

'Did she get better?' asked Sarah, looking at me and frowning.

'Yes. The leg mended, but it was never really straight again. And the worst thing was we had to keep moving: and the jolting of the wagon gave her no relief from the pain.'

William Jex's children
Back Row: Rosetta Caroline, Artemesia Jane, Ann Malinda, Hannah Eliza.
Front row: Alice Vilate, Emma Eliza, Sarah Ann.

It was hard for the women. They faced the same risks as the men and had to work as hard; even harder. When the little 'uns got tired of walking the mothers had to carry them on their backs. And when we had rivers to cross. That's why we tarred the underside of the wagons. Crossing rivers was the most dangerous part of the journey: wagons could float away on a strong current, dragging the panicking, bellowing oxen off their feet and drowning both them and the men struggling to control them. Oxen could not be replaced and if we lost some it meant that wagons had to be abandoned and their loads shared out among the others, and that caused them to wear out quicker and sooner or later they would break down.

William Phelps gathered the family headmen and spoke to us about the final stage of the journey. The Wasatch mountain range stood in front of the wagons and we had to go either north or south of it. North was shorter, but higher and could become snowbound in an early winter. But there was water and grazing. South had easier gradients but was longer and the grazing and water could be unreliable.

Before we made a decision Phelps told us about a wagon train headed by the Donner family who, the year before, had tried the northern route, intending to continue west to settle in California They'd had a lot of bad luck; oxen drowned, wagons falling apart and a very early winter. The wagons had become buried in snow in the Sierra Nevada and after a while the people began arguing among themselves over food supplies. Some set off on foot over the mountains to try to reach settlements on the other side. The others had to sit there in roughly made tents and cabins, trying to stay alive. But their food ran out and pretty soon they started to die. The others realised that the only way they could survive was by eating their dead companions. And that's what they did. A few of the survivors were found by rescue parties but altogether half the migrants died during that winter. Phelps let us talk among ourselves and then asked us to vote on which route we wanted to take. We decided to go north and the next morning a clear sky revealed to us the distant peaks of the Wasatch Mountains rising up like a wall from the prairie, the final barrier to be overcome

Phelps ordered two days of rest and prayer to prepare us for the last stages of the journey. The oxen were allowed to graze freely on the rich grass and the wagons were thoroughly checked over by the excited people. Everyone was thrilled and eager to get moving, but I got a shock.

My friend Horace Howlett - you remember him, Sarah. I told you I used to work for his father back in England?

21

Sarah nodded. 'His Pa gave Horace some money to make the trip.'

'That's him.'

Well, a couple of weeks before he'd been bitten by a tick and the wound went bad. He got what we called Mountain Fever. Phelps knew what it was, he'd seen it before you see. Horace got all the symptoms; rash that oozed blood, shortage of breath, joint pain and all the rest. Well, we tried everything we knew and prayed for him, but it was no good. And he died on the second day of our rest before the final stage of our journey. Before he passed, he asked me to do him a favor. Sounds crazy now, but it made sense at the time: he asked me, after he'd gone, to take off his boots: they were strong, English boots, good quality, and give them to someone who was badly shod. Just like him: always thinking of others. We buried him deep in front of the lead wagon, filled up the grave and said the words over him. Then Phelps ordered the wagons to start and the whole train; wagons, oxen, people, passed over the grave so that there was no sign of it. If we hadn't, the wolves would have dug him up or the Indians would have scalped his corpse.

I stood to one side of the wagons and watched as they passed by, the people nodding to me as they went, silent and respectful. I stood there for a few minutes, remembering my dear friend in life but rejoicing in his entry to the afterword and I knew I would see him again.

Chapter 5

January 21st 1926, Spanish Fork, Utah

You'll see from the date that I've not been keeping up with my story. Fact is I've been ill. Just a head cold but it's left me tired and feeling sorry for myself and I told Sarah, she's got a weak chest you know, to stay away to stop her getting what I've had. I'm well looked after though: one good thing about having so many kin living nearby is that I had plenty of food, firewood, you name it! Nephew Heber came last week with a loaf of bread straight out of the oven and a pot of his own honey. That was a real treat. I guess you know I've a sweet tooth.

Sarah's arrived! It's good to see her again. She's got her notebook and pencils and ready for the next part of my story. When she sits in the firelight her hair shines like spun gold. She sure is a handsome woman. She's looking at me surprised, but I think she likes a compliment. What woman doesn't?

Well, we'd reached the part where Horace Howlett had died, God rest his soul, and the wagons had rolled on until we reached the northern pass over the Wasatch mountains.

We had prepared well for the difficult mountain crossing although we sometimes had to double up the oxen to haul the wagons up the worst inclines. But after a week of hard labour, we finally crossed the ridge and had an easy passage down the eastern slopes into our new homeland: Zion, the basin of the Great Salt Lake. It was September 30, 1854, just eight years after our leader Brigham Young had brought the first settlers to this holy place. We held a special prayer meeting to give thanks for our safe arrival.

And then I had to get myself moving! First thing was to meet with the Permanent Emigration Society: the Church organisation that financed the Gathering, as we called the flow of people coming to Utah. I know now for a fact that the Church had become short of the money necessary to fit out the group that was planning to travel here the next year, 1855. They were told to use man hauled hand carts or even wheel barrows as the usual wagons could not be afforded that year. They made it!

I had used up all my money and had been loaned the rest by the Church. I had to pay it back and give a tenth of all I earned in the future. I built a cabin against the steep side of a hill and dug out the soil where the cabin met the cliff, put in some roof timbers and kept digging until we had a simple home. We had brushwood for beds and I even found a small pane of glass that I fixed in the cabin front so we could have some light.

I had to work some of the time as a labourer on the Church farm, and later I worked on the foundations of our Temple. This was as well as clearing my own patch of land near the Salt Lake. We were hungry all the time, although I received my wages – one dollar seventy-five a day – in food. It was never enough. Eliza worked as a teacher in the school and even sold what clothes she could do without. Many times, all we had to eat was boiled nettles. And Eliza was expecting by then.

All the time this was going on the settlers had to watch out for a band of Paiute Indians who were making trouble. You see, they'd always been hunters and spent their time roaming the plains looking for buffalo or any other game, and fighting with other tribes whenever their young men felt like proving themselves. They were proud and fierce and would take offence at anything. Then, when the white men came with their cattle the Indians couldn't resist the temptation to steal them; after all the animals were there for the taking weren't they?

Well, just before our group arrived in Salt Lake an Indian band led by Chief Wakara – we called him, Walker- had been invited by Mormon farmers to meet up and talk over the cattle thefts and try to get the Indians to mend their ways. Well, everything was fine until one of the farmers got riled up at the Indians' attitude that he pushed one off his horse. Big mistake! You don't insult an Indian like that and get away with it. Well, things got out of hand then and before it stopped two men -one of theirs; one of ours - were killed. That was in fifty-three, just a year before we arrived here. Fell right into the middle of a war.

Sarah looks up an' asked, 'What was Wakara really like. Was he bad as everyone says?'

I saw him in fifty-five, just before he died. Pneumonia. It was at the treaty signing. He was a big man: over six feet tall and strong as an ox. Used to paint his face yellow when he was leading his war band. The best shot in the tribes. He was a man to be treated with care. You want to know if he was a bad man. Well by our standards he was a murderer, a thief and a liar. But the Indians saw him different. He was a born leader, a man who would protect their way of life and keep the white men from taking over their land

"You still had a lot of trouble though?" Sarah asks. "Even after the signing?"

We always had trouble from them. Can't be trusted. Well, they were desperate; we were taking their land and they knew they'd starve if we weren't stopped".

"What happen at Mountain Meadows, Grandpa?"

The sudden question caught me unprepared.

"Who told you about that?" I snapped, speaking sharp. Sarah noticed that she'd touched on a sore spot.

"Somebody was whispering about it. Seemed like it's a big secret. Something bad happened, didn't it?"

I sat quiet for a while, thinking fast. I'd hoped that what happened up there in the mountains had been forgotten. But clearly someone who should have known better had been spreading rumours. I made my decision.

It began in Illinois, 1857. There was Mormon feller there. His name was Parley P. Pratt. Well, he was a single man and he admired a lady neighbour, Eleanor Mclean. Not a Mormon, but all the same a respectable married lady. Don't get me wrong. Her husband was pretty cruel to her: he abused her and did all sorts to her that no woman should have to put up with.

Well, the Mormon feller takes pity on her and starts to be friendly, in a neighbourly way and soon they become close and fall in love. She leaves her husband and goes to live with the Mormon. The husband is furious and goes to a Judge and demands that the Mormon returns his property - that's what he said, 'property'.

The Judge listened him out, spoke to the Mormon and then started to ask the wife for her side of the story. So she told the Judge had been going on between her and her husband, and the Judge threw the husband's claim out and told the woman she'd be better off with the Mormon.

Well, Pratt and the woman left the court happy, but soon ran into trouble. There was the usual anti Mormon feeling in the town and bunch of toughs didn't like the way the husband had been treated and started to threaten Pratt. He got so scared that he went to the sheriff and asked for protection. The sheriff obliged and locked the Mormon up in his prison cell. But he didn't lock the door very well and must have been looking the other way because that night the toughs entered the sheriff's office and shot the Mormon dead.

The newspapers got hold of the story and all took against Pratt and more or less said that he'd got what he deserved. The story got people riled up against the Mormons and whipped up anger against our practice of plural marriage especially in the eastern cities. Then the politicians got hold of it and the Republicans saw some easy votes by calling for Government action against us, talking about what they called 'the twin evils of Slavery and Polygamy'.

Well Sarah, you've got to realise that at the same time as this Pratt business was happening in Illinois, a wagon train was passing through the state on its way to California. It had started off in Arkansas in the spring of '57. A big party of migrants. Not Mormons like us, but well to do folks, wealthy, some of them. They were aiming to make their fortunes in the gold fields of California. That was a six-month journey in those days. It was headed by two family groups; the Bakers and the Fanchers. There were 150 men, women and children. They had 40 wagons and over 1000 oxen and a lot of horses. These people picked up the story of the Pratt murder as they were passing through Illinois and spread the gossip as they travelled west.

The Baker Fancher party reached Utah after about three months of travel, but needed to resupply from the stores in Salt Lake City, which by that time had become a major trading post on the California trail. But then their trouble started. The hot heads in the party had been spreading the gory details of the Pratt murder and news of their boasting had reached our leader Brigham Young. He issued an order that as punishment, the Arkansas migrants were not to be supplied with anything but neither were they to be harmed in any way.

When they were told that they would be sold no more fresh supplies, the migrants got real mad and became even more offensive. They deliberately poisoned the wells when they left their overnight camps and started to say bad things about our Church and its leaders. Now, I was in Salt Lake City one day for the baptism of my daughter – she was eight years old and ready - and I heard the great Heber C Kimball preaching about the instructions which our Church's founder, the Prophet Joseph Smith, had given us before he was assassinated. His words were burned into my brain and have stayed with me and guided me all my life. I'm sure he said, plain and simple, that the enemies of our religion should be killed, just as the Apostles had killed Judas. Kimber swore that it was true because Saint Peter had spoken with him and had told him so himself. Then, a few days later, one of those evil people, those migrant Godless devils, stood up on his wagon, raised a rifle and shouted,

'I've got the gun that shot the guts out of your old Jo Smith.'

That evil man could not have been more offensive: a wave of anger swept over the whole Mormon community and those migrants didn't know how close they'd come to being lynched. Before we'd settled in Utah, we'd been the minority people – in Illinois, Mississippi, even back in England, everywhere, and we'd had to take the insults, the beatings, the killings, the sheer damned injustice! But here? No! This was our land, paid for in tears, sweat and blood. We had built it up from nothing: we were in charge. But Brigham Young had ordered that we must not attack those vermin and our discipline held. But Sarah, I can't tell you how difficult it was to obey that order.

By that time, like most men over the age of 15 in that part of the country, I had joined the Mormon Militia and was prepared to serve in a locally raised company, commanded by Andrew Bart which was part of John Sharp's battalion. We were all prepared to take on those detested migrants, but the order from Brigham Young never came. I realised that I was feeling cold: the afternoon sun had no heat in it. I put a couple of logs on the fire.

The migrants continued travelling south through Utah, hoping to find some outlying settlement or even Mexican traders in order to buy the supplies so that they could continue their journey to California. And then they reached Mountain Meadows. It was a piece of high land, pretty level and bitter cold in winter, but good summer grazing. Then, without warning, a large force of Indians – mostly Paiutes – opened fire on them from prepared positions – an unusual tactic for Indians, who were well armed with modern weapons, probably traded from the Mexicans for horses. The migrants began to take casualties as they frantically tried to circle their wagons and get their people under cover.

They were in a bad position; wide open to attack, without natural cover and most important, without water. They sent out two fast riders, heading north, towards Mormon settlements to call for men to help them. The riders easily avoided the Indians and got away. The Indians kept up an effective fire and the fight went on for 4 days until the migrants had almost given up hope and were expecting to have to fight to the last man. They were desperate for water, were running short of ammunition and had dozens of wounded men, women and children.

But help arrived at the last minute: a force of Mormon Militia was seen to be riding into the Indian positions under a flag of truce. The Indians stopped shooting and some could be seen talking to the Militia officers. Then two soldiers, one of them was Militia Commander John D. Lee, rode towards the migrant wagons under the same flag and announced that they had persuaded the Paiutes to stop their attack and let the migrants go on their way. But the Indians insisted that the migrants gave up their wagons, horses, oxen and weapons. The terms were accepted: the migrants knew they were beaten and realised that the California dream was over, but at least they would escape with their lives, as the Militiamen promised to protect them.

And so it was that the migrants left the protection of the circled wagons and walked out into the open ground of the Mountain Meadows: the men in the first column, then the women and older children and finally two wagons filled with wounded and the smallest children and babies. Armed militiamen marched protectively on the flanks of the columns. As soon as the second wagon had left the deserted camp the Militia Commander, Lee, shouted, 'Militia, do your duty!' The men obeyed the order and turned their weapons on the defenceless migrants. All but eleven, the youngest children and babes in arms, were shot down and killed: One hundred-and forty men women and children. The Indians joined in the killing and murdered the badly wounded in the wagons

Sarah looked at me, horrified. 'That can't be true. Our men wouldn't do such a wicked thing! 'Wicked? Maybe,' I replied. 'But that's what they did. And I'm not finished yet. Keep writing. I want the truth to be known. All of it.'

I paused a moment, looking at that fire and saw that it wasn't burning well: summer cut timber makes poor firewood.

The Mountain Meadows Massacre

Painted to depict a mass murder which Mormons blamed on Native Americans and has now been described as '*the most hideous example of the human cost exacted by religious fanaticism in American history until 9/11*' It was a mass murder for which Mormons, who were in fact the main culprits, tried unsuccessfully to blame Native Americans.

'Sarah, it was an act from start to finish. The migrants were fooled.'

She frowned, 'What do you mean?

'I mean some of the so-called Indians were white men - Mormons! Disguised to look like Indians, they even stained their faces and wore Indian clothes. Commander Lee had it all planned from start to finish. That was why the so-called Indians had fought with modern weapons and white soldiers' tactics. The migrants swallowed it whole! The two riders who went off looking for help were allowed to escape so that they would spread the word that the migrants were being attacked by

Indians. Lee could say later that he had got to the Mountain Meadows too late to help.

'So what happened next?' asked Sarah.

'The bodies were stripped of clothing, jewellery, anything that could identify those people. They were buried in shallow graves where they had fallen. The youngest little 'uns – the youngest was less than a year old – were taken to nearby Mormon settlements to be brought up in our faith. The weapons were shared out among the attackers and all the other stuff was sold by auction. Lee took the oxen, wagons and most of the horses.'

We sat silent for a while, Sarah pale and tearful after what I had told her. She looked up. 'You were a militiaman, Grandpa. Were you there? Part of it? The killing?'

'No: that was done by others and my Company wasn't ordered to take part.'

'Yes, but would --------'

'I'm tired,' I said, interrupting her quickly. 'I think that's enough for now. I'm going to have an early night.

1850s Mormon Militiamen

Chapter 6

February 19ᵗʰ 1926, Spanish Fork, Utah

I haven't been well these last couple of weeks: bad cold again and my chest hurts. The weather's no help neither. All this snow and freezing winds. I don't move much from the fire. Doc came to see me yesterday. Gave me a bottle of something to ease the cough, but it hasn't done much good yet. We used to do pretty well without doctors years ago: just relied on the old ways.

I remember when we were on the Plains on our way here in '54, a lady in one of the wagons had just had a baby and was having trouble feeding it: she had this real nasty discharge from her breasts and her baby wouldn't suck and began to lose weight, crying all the time. Course we had no doctor, but a lady called Mrs. Atkinson had seen something like it back in England and said she knew how to cure the poor woman. Well, Mrs. A. went and borrowed a new born puppy from some folks whose collie bitch had just had a litter of fine healthy pups and borrowed one. She took it to the sick woman and put the puppy to the worst affected breast and the puppy sucked all the discharge away. Cleared it up just fine! Mrs. A. said it was something in the pup's saliva that did the trick. Anyway, it worked and the baby, a girl, thrived, and 17 years later I officiated at her wedding.

But enough of that. I've got some explaining to do when Sarah comes; I know I upset her last time when I cut her short and finished the story-telling early. I'm going to tell her the truth... She's walking in now and stamping he snow off her boots. I'll let her get settled and then come clean.

She came in and I took her coat and sat her near the fire. I spoke gentle to her.

'The last time you were here I told you about the Mountain Meadows massacre.'

Sarah nodded her head.

'And you were going to ask me a question.'

She nodded again.

'You were going to ask if I would have taken part in those killings if I'd been ordered to. Yes?'

'That's right Grandpa. Would you?'

'Sarah, I've asked myself that question a hundred times; would I have obeyed my Militia commander or my conscience? You've got to understand; they were desperate times. Those evil people were really hated and we felt threatened on all sides. Well, I've got to tell you that even so, I hope I would have refused to take part. But all the same I'm mighty pleased the Lord didn't put me to the test. After the war, the war against the South I mean, Lee, the Militia Commander responsible was found guilty of murder in a Federal court and executed by firing squad.'

'I'm sure he deserved it. And you're a good man, Grandpa.' Sarah smiled at me and I knew I'd been right to be open with her.

'Well, there were others felt like me and anyway we soon had other things to think about. Mail riders reached Salt Lake City from the East with news that a large United States army unit was heading our way. Our Governor, Brigham Young, believed that that U.S. army was going to take over our homeland and destroy our way of life. They'd never liked our independent spirit and especially objected to plural marriage. Said it was un-American, whatever that meant.'

Sarah shook her head,

'Why couldn't they just leave us alone?' She didn't expect an answer; we both knew all too well how much the rest of the country disliked us.

We suspected that the approaching soldiers were going to attempt to kill us all and destroy our religion. This was just after the murder of Parley Pratt. Remember him? You can't imagine how much we were hated. Governor Brigham Young decided that he needed hard facts and sent two men out to be spies. Those fellers rode east until they found the soldiers. They had a story ready: said they were travelling from California and were going home back east after finding little gold and a heap of trouble. They were made welcome by the soldiers - a rough, foul-mouthed lot - and discovered that Brigham Young had been right to take the threat seriously. They openly boasted to the spies that when they reached Utah their officers would give them a free hand to destroy, rape and murder without restraint and were keen to begin their wicked work.

The spies returned to Salt Lake City and gave the information to Governor Young who straight away set in motion a well-prepared plan; all militia men were ordered to settle their family affairs and report to their Company Commanders as soon as they could and take up positions to stop the soldiers invading Utah.

'So that's how you got involved, Grandpa.'

'That was how we all got into it; every man over fifteen was involved in the end.'

But first I had to move my family and I only had a few days to do it. Our home then was north of Salt Lake City: a timber cabin and a neat farm. But it was right in the path of an invading army coming from the north east – that's what the spies had found out. I had to move them quick, so I loaded up my wagon with Eliza, the girls and the few bits and pieces of furniture and farm tools we had collected. We had three daughters then; Sarah Ann, she was, let me think, seven years old, then Emma Eliza 3, and Alice Vilate 1. And Eliza was expecting Rosetta Caroline. I was heartbroken to leave our home and the farm. We all wept but it had to be done and I never saw them again: Governor Brigham Young ordered that the foreign soldiers, as he called them, should find nothing to help them if they invaded our homeland, and everything had to be removed or destroyed: crops, houses, animals, forage, all had to go including our home. Our enemies would find a waste land.

I found a place to rent for my family. Just temporary, until the threat of invasion was over, in a little place called Spanish Fork. Only a small place; it had been a staging post on the old Spanish trail overland from the Caribbean coast to California. You smile Sarah. Yes, that's when we arrived here and although I thought we wouldn't be staying long, we've been here ever since. Well, I unloaded the wagon, got all the family into their new home – just a couple of rooms at a friend's place: George Washington Sevy. I'll never forget him. He and his wife Phoebe were like brother and sister to Eliza and me. Good old George: he had to high tail it down to Mexico in eighty-five when the Federal marshals found out he'd taken a third wife and made no secret of it, just when they were trying to stamp polygamy out.

Sarah stopped writing and held up her hand to stop me.

'Why did the Federal men pick on him, Grandpa? There must have been lots of others with plural wives: even you at one time.'

'Yes, well, you see there wasn't much anybody could do practically about the men who'd had lots of wives for a long time. If they put the parents in jail what would happen to the little 'uns? So they just told them to keep their heads down and they let sleeping dogs lie. But my friend George had married number three openly, in defiance, you might say. Had himself a great celebration and invited all his friends – me included. Well, the marshals had to do something and nearly caught him. But he got away into Mexico. He's dead now.'

I gave Eliza all the money I had to hand: just a few dollars. She was upset at the upheaval and told me so. She wasn't a sharp-spoken woman usually, but she sure let me know she was truly riled. 'You're leaving me very badly provided for, Billy,' she said. But she had to accept things, same as me. We both knew that we might not live through the next few months.

I stayed with the family for an hour or so to see them settled, then left and went back to Salt Lake City. I sold the wagon and team there. There were plenty of buyers: hundreds of folks wanted to head away from the likely invasion points. I bought me a Kentucky rifle and reported to the Militia mustering depot. There were lots of us, and a strange crew we looked; not a uniform to be seen, all ages and carrying our own weapons – all sorts of guns. A blacksmith had been turning scythes and ploughshares into bayonets and had even made a few copies of Mr. Colt's revolver, but I wouldn't guarantee they'd be safe to use: probably damage the guy pulling the trigger more than the other feller.

By August 1, 1857 the muster was complete: our various Companies had been formed and we were ordered to move off to our   positions. We knew that the U.S. soldiers, under a General Johnson, planned to invade the Salt Lake Basin from the east through the canyons and that was where we were going to stop them. First thing was to dam the rivers at the mouth of the canyons. This would flood the low ground in the valley bottoms and force the invaders to crowd up when they were forced to go round the floods –that would make them easier targets. Next, we dug rifle pits across the canyons where the soil was thick and on the sloping hill sides, we built breastworks of rocks. We cut down any trees or shrubs which would give the enemy cover. Finally, we measured the land and put in distance markers so that our riflemen could aim accurately. Just a few men could defend those canyons pretty easy.

We kept riders watching the army as it slowly moved west towards us. President Buchanan had sent two thousand five hundred men - about one fifth of the entire U.S. army - against us. And that was his biggest mistake.

Sarah stopped writing and looked up, frowning.

'How come? Surely a big army was better for them.'

I nodded and put a couple of logs on the fire.

'You'd be right most of the time, but then, you see, such a large number of soldiers needed a lot of supplies. Remember, they had to travel a thousand miles from their base in Kansas to reach us and that called for a lot of wagons, oxen, mules and spare horses. That huge wagon train of supplies, moving at the speed of the slowest ox team was their weakness: the leader, General Johnson, allowed his soldiers - all on horseback - to get ahead of the supply train and split the army in two.'

Sarah's frown disappeared.

'And that wasn't a good idea?'

I laughed.

'Worst thing he could have done. We had one of the smartest men I've ever known, Major Lot Smith, in charge of the Mormon militia shadowing Johnson's army. He had 43 men and decided to attack the defenceless wagon trains."

'Were you one of the 43 men, Grandpa?' asked Sarah.

'No, I'd liked to have been, but Lot Smith wanted men born to the saddle and I never was that good a rider. I was told to help defend the valleys leading into Utah from the east, especially because of that Kentucky rifle I'd bought in Salt Lake City.'

'Yes, I wanted to ask you before; what was so special about a Kentucky rifle – you mentioned it earlier.'

I smiled at her.'

'It was a rifle; had spiral grooves inside a real long barrel. Very accurate it was: a man could shoot the eye out of a squirrel at 200 yards, if he knew what he was doing.

'Did you ever kill anyone with it?'

'No. Not then. Not white men. But later in the Black Hawk Rebellion in '65 I shot a few Indians; but they don't count. Anyway Sarah, I'm getting off the point: I was telling you about Major Lot Smith.'

She nodded and I carried on with the story.

Lot was a great friend of mine. About the same age, and he told me himself about what he did. He's dead now; like so many of 'em. Died in ninety-two or ninety-three; can't remember exactly, but he was one in a million: brave as a lion and one of the best frontiersmen in the West. He had a great sense of humour, you know. Told me once that when he needed a new pair of boots he'd go into the store and buy the biggest pair they had so he'd get value for money. I still miss him.

Well, Lot had been keeping a close watch on the wagon train from a distance; he didn't want the U.S. soldiers to know that the Mormons had a strong force nearby. He found out that there were no soldiers with the wagons, just civilian drivers – and a rough bunch they were! There were 25 wagons, each hauled by a 6 team of oxen and driven by a single bullwhacker. Well, Lot struck at first light one morning: he and his men rode quietly into the circled wagons and began to take over. They disarmed the drivers while half of them were still asleep – they only had a few sidearms. You would have laughed, Sarah; one of the drivers was supposed to ring a handbell to warn of any attack, but the feller who was responsible for ringing it couldn't find it and Lot's men dragged him out of his wagon before he'd had time to get his britches on.

Only one of the bullwhackers, feller called Simpson, tried to resist; came flying out of his wagon like a scalded cat and yelled, "I'll skin you alive, your whoreson, Hell spawned bastards", but when he saw that he was up against Lot Smith he caved in and handed over his weapon. Lot Smith had a reputation even then as a very dangerous enemy: he'd made quite a name for himself in the Mexican war in '46 – '48. Anyway, Simpson calmed down and asked Lot what was going to happen.

'That depends on you,' said Smith.

'How do you mean?' asked Simpson.

'On whether your contract with the Army says you're hired to fight or drive wagons.'

Simpson didn't want any misunderstanding and was quick to answer. "We're just drivers, Major. Not soldiers. We don't want no trouble. We'll just turn our wagons round and get out of your way."

'No. You got the last bit right, but you're not taking those wagons. I'm going to burn them." He paused. 'You going to stop me?

Simpson looked shocked. 'No sir, but can I ask you something, please?'

Lot nodded.

'One of them wagons belong to my Pa in Law. He's not a wealthy man and if he loses his wagon, it'll ruin him.'

Smith thought for a moment and then told Simpson that he could keep two wagons to carry enough food, and stuff to get the drivers back east. And if he saw any of them again, he would shoot them down like dogs. The drivers believed that Smith was serious and did as they were told.

Sarah looked up and smiled. 'Well, I reckon that Major Smith was a very nice man; to let those poor bullwhackers go like that.'

I shook my head and matched her smile.

'He wasn't being kind: he was obeying orders. Brigham Young had told him not to kill anyone if he could possibly help it. He wanted the government, the newspaper men and especially the ordinary people

– the voters back east, to see that we Mormons were peaceful, hard-working folk who meant no harm to anyone, who just wanted to live our lives and practise our religion. And his plan worked: the newspapers in the big cities started to show some sympathy for our cause and the government got worried that they would lose support from the voters.

'Well, I still think he was a kind man', said Sarah stubbornly.

I had to laugh. 'can assure you that the U.S. government didn't call him that. Lot went on that fall to destroy 2 more wagon trains carrying supplies to their army. Over a hundred wagons and half a million pounds of supplies were taken. The government put a $1,000 bounty on Smith, dead or alive, but nobody never got near him. Lot Smith's work pretty well ruined the army's plans: they now weren't able to invade Utah and fight a lengthy campaign against determined and well-prepared Mormon forces – we had about 2,000 armed men waiting for them, all of us ready to defend our sacred homeland with our lives. Neither could they turn around and go a thousand miles back into Kansas – they would starve; no cold weather clothing, nothing to eat. So they decided to go north a little way into Wyoming and winter there. They found shelter of sorts in an old ruined fort and spent a miserable winter there. Cold and hungry, poor devils. 400 of them deserted, I remember.'

Then my cough came back and I had to stop talking for a while. Sarah put the kettle on the fire and made me a cup of chamomile tea with a little honey in it. There's some folks don't approve of anything but water, but I reckon it's medicine. It eased my cough and I carried on with the story.

As soon as the threat from Johnson's army had gone, Brigham Young sent a message to the U.S. Government proposing a peace deal. He knew that although things were going well for us at that time, in the long run we would be invaded and war would ruin our precious land. Young also knew that the Government was worried about the prospect of full-scale war with the South over slavery. If that happened the U.S. would have two wars to fight at the same time: one in the south and another a thousand miles away in the west.

Sarah smiled and looked up from her notebook. 'So was there a peace treaty?'

39

'Yes. Both sides had too much to lose and both had to give way a little. We had to accept a Federally appointed Governor, but that didn't worry us much: we looked on Brigham Young, the head of the Church, as our leader and pretty well ignored the Government man. And we allowed a token unit of U.S. troops occupy a fort on condition that they didn't interfere with the way we wanted to live.'

'That sounds reasonable,' said Sarah. 'What did the U.S. give up?'

'They had to abandon their plans to invade Utah and set up their own Godless government here. That let them build up their forces to prepare for the expected war with the South.'

'Thank the Lord for common sense,' said Sarah. 'It could have been a terrible tragedy.'

Dugout house with wood framed opening (Butcher 1886)

Settlers' house 1890

Chapter 7

March 2nd 1926, Spanish Fork, Utah

Sarah came early today. I'm pleased she did because I needed the company and I was pretty low.

You know what it's like after a bad head cold. It leaves you feeling weak and you can't be bothered to do anything? Well, that's been me for a couple of weeks now. I'd gotten real down, feeling sorry for myself. And then we had a bitter blow that really knocked the stuffing out of us: one of my great grandchildren got herself killed. Little Elizabeth. Youngest daughter of grandson John William and Effie. She was only seven years old and got knocked down in the street by an automobile. The driver never stopped and nobody can say who he was or say for sure what sort of vehicle it was except that it could have been a Ford, model T. But you know as well as I do, there's hundreds of them Tin Lizzies around - been making them for years.

Our local doctor was called to her pretty quick, but poor little Elizabeth was unconscious and never came round: a bad head injury. Folks who saw it happen gathered round and prayed for her, but it was no good and she passed into Paradise right there in the street. Her Ma, Young Effie, came to me later that day and asked if Elizabeth would be happy in the Afterlife and who would look after her; would she stay being a little girl through Eternity or would she be allowed to grow up, get married there and know the love of a good man. As a priest of the Church, I had to tell her that Paradise was such a wonderful place that ordinary mortals like us couldn't possibly understand what happens there, but she could be sure that the Lord would take her into his care and in his good time Effie would see her daughter again. She seemed to find my words comforting and went home.

Sarah frowned and shook her head.

"I can't never understand why the Lord should take a child from her parents. My son was killed in the '17/18 war but he knew the risk he was taking when he volunteered. But poor little Elizabeth! It's not fair."

I held my hand up to stop her. "Don't let thoughts like that get into your head, Sarah. It means that your faith is being tested by the

Evil One. Be strong and know that the Lord has called the child to himself because her time has come. Be strong Sarah."

She sighed and wiped a tear from her face. '

'Yes, I know. I mustn't let myself think like that.' She paused. "We'd better carry on where we left off last time?'

'Yes. I think so. We're getting on pretty well,' I said.

Sarah smiled and asked,

'When are you going to talk about your other wife?'

Sometime this morning, if we get going. Put a couple of logs on the fire and I'll begin.

'First thing though, I must talk a little about is the War between the North and the South. '61 to '65. The marriage and the children and the War; they all happened at the same time, see?' I paused and smiled to myself. I raised my eyes and looked at Sarah. 'Brigham Young was a truly great man. You know why?'

Sarah shook her head.

'Because he kept us out of the War,' I said. 'We didn't like slavery and lots of folks sympathised with the North, but Brigham Young was dead against us getting involved, especially when the Government asked for our soldiers. He was the head of our Church and more of a leader than any Northern politician. Remember, Sarah, the North hadn't protected the Mormons from the riots and killings in Illinois, and had let our founder, Joseph Smith, be assassinated in '44. They'd even sent Buchannan's army against us in '58. We owed them nothing! Brigham Young wrote a piece in the 'Deseret Times' that I recall; "I'll see them in Hell before I raise an army for them, 'he said. That sure told them.'

'The War was terrible, grandpa,' said Sarah, frowning. 'Folks still tell stories about it.'

'Folk should get on their knees every day and thank the Lord for Brigham Young's vision and courage in keeping us out of it. Do you know something, in one of the battles, at a place called Gettysburg, the North lost thousands of men killed? Thousands! And the crazy thing was, the Northern Generals said that they had won a great victory because the South had lost more! If we had sent our Mormon boys to help the North and if we had lost thousands killed, our homeland here in Utah, our Zion, would have died out.'

I paused for a few moments as a coughing fit overtook me. Sarah looked up, concerned.

'I'm all right Sarah,' I managed to say after a while. 'My chest's been playing me up lately. Let's carry on.'

The War between the North and the South dragged on and left us alone, and we prospered! The railroads brought in more settlers, more land went under the plough and my lumber business made me a wealthy man. During the War the annual turnover at the Lumber Yard hit $100,000 for the first time! Folks didn't want to live in dugouts or log cabins any more: they wanted bigger, timber framed houses and the demand for sawn timber from the Jex Lumber Company just kept getting bigger. My family got bigger too in those years; Artamesia Jane had been born just as the War started and then Eliza had Richard Henry, George Hyrum, and Anna Malinda during the war years.

Jemima Cox Jex

And then, on January 5th, 1865, right at the end of the War, I took a second wife. Her name was Jemima Cox. She was 29 years old when I married her. English born. Came from a place called Leicester. She'd been a worker in a hosiery factory and had converted to the Mormon faith in 1857, borrowed enough money from the Emigration Fund and came to Utah in the fall of '62. She was always proud of the fact that she had paid back all the money she had borrowed for her journey from the Fund a lot quicker than most folks. She was a hard worker. I got to know her when she was doing housework for a neighbour.

'What did you say to her, Grandpa?' asked Sarah with a smile.

'Well, I just told her that I thought she would be a good wife for me and I would be good for her. I told her that I was a successful man and could afford to set her up in a comfortable house. I was a well-respected member of the Church. I had fathered eight children with Eliza and never a cripple among them and would be a good father to her children.'

'And she said yes? said Sarah, frowning.

'Of course, she did,' I replied. 'It was a good offer. We had to marry quietly though, without any fuss: I didn't want some Federal marshal chasing me with a bigamy charge. We married in Salt Lake City in January, 1865. My friend Erasmus Snow officiated and our witness was William Phelps.'

'What did your other wife, Eliza, think about Jemima? Did they become friends?'

'As far as I was concerned, I expected them to behave like sisters. They never became close, but they knew what was expected of them and there was never any trouble. Anyway, not when I was around. But I sometimes used to wish that they were friendlier to each other.'

'I heard that the marriage didn't last long.' said Sarah, gently. The way she spoke, it was more like a question.

'That's right,' I replied. 'Our earthly marriage didn't last long but our Celestial marriage had been sealed for Eternity, just like mine and Eliza's had been. We'll meet again in Paradise eventually.'

'You had children with her, though'

'Yes. In the fall of 1865, we had William George. But he died a few months later. Next there was James Henry in '67, Jemima Sophia in '69 and David Walter in '72. Then Jemima herself died in 1877. Gallstones, the doctor said it was as nasty a case as he'd ever come across.'

'What happened to her children?'

'Why, I just run 'em in with mine and Eliza's. Eliza didn't mind none. Didn't cause too much problem because two years later the oldest two, Jemima Sophia and James Henry died within a month of

44

each other. Diphtheria. Jemima Sophia was 10 years old and James Henry was 12. David Walter died later in '85 when he was thirteen years old. He'd never have come to much; a weak, sickly child. Eliza did what she could for Jemima's little 'uns, but she had her hands full with her own babes. We had Hannah Eliza and John William - twins - in '67 and Heber Charles in '71. Yes, those were good years for us. Bountiful harvests, lots of little 'uns and everyone seemed to be prosperous. There was only one problem.'

'What was that?' asked Sarah.

'The Indians. Their chief, Black Hawk, began attacking Mormon settlements; killing and burning. And they soon struck against us. But I'll tell you about that next time. My chest hurts now.'

Corporal, 3rd US Infantry
1846

Lt. Colonel, 11th US Infantry
1847

2nd Lieutenant, 4th US Infantry
1847

1st Sergeant, 8th US Infantry
1847

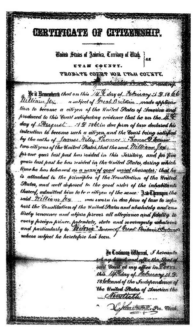

Full readable copy of this document on page 62

Full readable copy of this document on page 63

Mormon Leader, Brigham Young

Eliza had always been uncomfortable with the fact that, in the eyes of the Church of England, her Mormon marriage to William on the dockside at Liverpool was illegal under Anglican Church law. So they married again in Salt Lake City in 1892, where their union became official. Note that Eliza gives her original maiden name as 'Eliza Goodson

Chapter 8

March 9th 1926, Spanish Fork, Utah

Ipromised Sarah last week that I would tell her about the trouble we had with the Indians in the late 60s. There'd been some killing and cattle rustling for as long as I could remember but it had been gradually getting worse. I reckon that the Civil War had been the cause – in Utah, especially. You see, while the Whites had been busy killing each other, neither side had been able to keep the Indians in their place. As a result, the raids had gotten worse. Particularly in Utah. We were on our own here; the Government had never wanted to help us – even before the War with the South. They didn't like our way of life and remember; we'd made them look pretty small when we saw off President Buchanan's soldiers when they'd tried to attack us. By rights though, they should have helped because we were still just a Territory of the United States at that time: their responsibility.

Sarah's come in now. Stamping the snow off her boots. I've got the kettle boiling and we'll have a cup of camomile tea. She likes it and it's good for my chest.

'I've gotten a taste for your camomile tea, Grandpa.' she said as she bustled into my kitchen. 'Mind if I put a little of honey in it?'

'Help yourself Sarah.' I replied, pointing to the cupboard by the window.

'You're going to talk about the Indian troubles. That right?'

'That's right. Soon as you've got yourself settled by the fire.'

She brought her tea over and we sat companionably and sipped our hot drinks. I put my cup down and said, 'I don't want you to think that there were great battles between us and whole tribes like Custer's fight on the Little Big Horn. For us here in Spanish Fork it was all on a small scale, but still very deadly. And we had to deal with it ourselves.'

Sarah opened her notebook, took a pencil from her pocket and looked at me expectantly.

In the Spring of 1866 Chief Black Hawk gathered together a bunch of renegades and trouble-makers. Paiutes mostly and a few

Shoshones and Crees. They had horses and weapons – what they hadn't stolen they'd bought from the Mexicans - and began attacking outlying farms; burning, taking cattle and horses and killing anyone who got in their way. Nobody was safe anymore. I reckon you'll get a clear picture if I tell you about one raid in particular. I was involved, so were a whole lot of local men: most are dead now though.

It was late in May that year if I remember right. There was a family, name of Givens, had a homestead just a little way out of town in Thistle Valley. You know where I mean?'' Sarah just nodded her head, scribbling away as fast as she could.

Well, this bunch of Indians caught Givens in his own yard by surprise. Killed him and his wife and their four children. Stole some cattle and rode off, thinking they'd got away with it. But they hadn't!... There were two young fellers passing through who'd been helping Givens – can't remember their names – any way, it don't matter none. These two fellers had been moving cattle out of the valley bottoms and up onto higher land. They'd seen it all happen. They hid in the willows by the creek and recognised some of the Indians. The two fellers were unarmed, well outnumbered and couldn't stop what was happening.

We call it now the 'West Field', Sarah. Know where I mean?

'I know it,' said Sarah, smiling. 'Pretty place; Tom and I used to go there before we were married.'

'Yes, well, those Indians stole cattle and horses from there, and as well they took more from William Berry's pasture. At daylight we discovered the thefts and saw that the thieves' tracks led towards Springfield Canyon. We returned to town, raised a squad under the leadership of William Creer. William was a leading man in the town and he said we had the right to take the law into our own hands and arrest the Indians. He said we were a posse comitatus, the authority of the community, and need not be afraid to kill the Indians if necessary, if they resisted.

There were sixteen of us, all determined to stop those Indian raids, even though we were poorly armed and two of us had no weapons at all. We followed the Indians' trail over Springfield Canyon, or Maple Canyon as it was known then. There we discovered the smouldering fire of the Indians' camp. We stopped for a while and took council as to our next movement and decided we must be most careful to guard against being taken by surprise through the cunning of the red man.

We followed the trail over what is known as Diamond Ridge and down into the canyon to the south, known as Diamond Fork Canyon. We decided to take the south side of the canyon and get in front of the stolen cattle and horses to prevent the Indians escaping with them. When half way down the canyon we came in sight of the Indians. We found that they had not anticipated being followed, and scented no trouble. They had unsaddled their horses and had turned them out to graze and were themselves busily engaged in preparing another 'feed'. They had roped a young steer and were in the act of butchering it when we gave the alarm to attack.

Colonel Creer aimed to impress the Indians with the fact that we meant business; in other words, we were to run the biggest bluff as possible, since our company was small and we were poorly prepared to put up much of a fight. The Indians immediately made for the brush along the creek, while we moved southward to get below them. While we were crossing the open ground, they opened fire. One bullet lodged in the shoulder of George Ainge's horse, so we knew that we were within range and that their shots might prove effective. We took our stand on a prominent point and firing became general on both sides.

A brother, Albert Dimmock, walked to the brow of the hill to make a survey of the field when one of the Indians who had crawled nearer to our position, fired, hit Dimmock in the stomach and he fell to the ground. John Koyle reached him and raised him up. I joined Koyle and opened Dimmock's clothes to see where the wound was located and discovered blood flowing from the lower part of his body. I knew that he was badly wounded; there was no wound on his back and we reckoned that the bullet must have lodged in his spine after passing through his belly. Others of the brethren came and we did what we could to relieve his pain, for he was suffering greatly. He begged us not to leave him, for he feared that the Indian who had shot him desired nothing so much as his scalp. We assured him that we would stay by him in all events.

It was pretty hot and poor Dimmock began to plead for water, as wounded men often do, but we had none to give him and it wasn't possible to get to the creek as the Indians occupied that position. Dimmock became hot and feverish. The firing continued for three or four hours, when we discovered, to our great delight that help was coming; reinforcements joined us and the firing became more intense. One of the new men, John Groesbeck, had trouble controlling his horse which was frightened by the firing. It bucked, the saddle twisted round and the rider was thrown to the ground. The horse ran off into the brush and the saddle and a new pistol attached to it were lost. At the same time brother Edmundson who was close behind Groesbeck, was shot and fell to the ground. I saw an Indian on the trail of Edmundson and concluded that he had gotten away like Groesbeck had. When he didn't make an appearance, we tried to find him but did not do so until the next morning when we found his body. He had been shot and killed. He had been scalped and one hand had been cut off at the wrist.

After the arrival of the reinforcements, the Indians began to move off. We saw them crossing the divide towards Soldier Fork on the south. Our first concern, after the firing ceased, was to get our wounded comrade to water. Two others and myself were ordered to stand guard to give the alarm, should the Indians return and renew the attack. The wounded man was carried to the creek where water was to be had. As soon as we felt that the skirmish was over and the Indians were in retreat, we set to work to provide a litter, which was made of ropes stretched between two poles running parallel, so that four men could carry him. Dimmock suffered intensely and begged us to lay him down to rest and die, but of course we could not do that. Before leaving, some of the boys gathered up the cattle that had been stolen by the Indians, which numbered about forty in all. The Indians had gotten away with some horses.

It was dusk when we finally reached town and got our wounded man to a doctor. It was found that – as we thought- the Indian's bullet had passed through Dimmock's bowels and lodged in his spine. After three days of terrible suffering, he died and so was among those who gave their lives to assist in the forward progress of Western civilization and development.

Patriarch, William Jex, far right and matriarch, Eliza (Goodson) Jex far left, bottom row.

Their children on the back row are Sarah Ann, Hannah Eliza, John William, Helen Charles, Richard Henry, George Hyrum, Ann Melinda and Alice Vilate. Their children on the front row are Rosetta Caroline, Artemesia Jane and Emma Elixa.

Early Jex family reunion

Jex Lumber Co,
Spanish Fork, Utah
(left and below)

Farm Scene, Mapleton, Utah

52

Salt Lake City's streetcar system near Main and Second.
(unattributed)

The urban communities of the late nineteenth century attempted to incorporate mass-transit systems into existing highway grids. The streets of Salt Lake City were designed for a team of oxen to turn a wagon round and were therefore provided commodious routes for the City's streetcar system.

Jex Broom Factory,
Spanish Fork, Utah
(above)

Chapter 9

April 11th 1926, Spanish Fork, Utah

Thank the good Lord the winter is over and my old bones don't hurt so much. Rheumatism, the doc says. Got to expect some aches and pains at my time of life, but I truly thank the Lord for the warm weather coming back.

Sarah's here early today. We haven't had any of our trips down memory lane lately – late frosts and heavy snow fall kept folk indoors as much as they could. So, I had plenty of time to think about things. Pretty lonely at times. Tell you what though; young Anderson came to bring me a load of firewood and stayed for a while to warm up by the fire. Now, he told me that he'd heard of a feller in England, name of Bard or Bird or some such: can't remember the name exactly. I forget things so easy.

'Now Sarah, what was I saying?'

'You were telling me about Mr. Bard or Bird, Grandpa.'

'He's very helpful, young Sarah. Yes, that feller in England. Well Anderson told me that Bard or whoever had invented a kind of box that showed moving pictures. Not like the movies, but sort of gathering the pictures from the air. Real living pictures showing things miles away. Folks can sit there and see what's going on someplace else. He called his picture machine a televizor and said his invention would change the world. Can't see it myself: who'd want to spend their life looking at pictures in a box? It'll never take on.

Anyway Sarah, I want to get started on this last part of my story. I'm going to skip a lot of recent stuff. I guess I'm well enough known by now that folks don't need telling what I've been up to these last few years; the timber business has prospered and I've become a wealthy man, I've seen the State has grown and gotten richer as well. You know all about me being a water bailiff and settling some pretty fierce disputes about access to irrigation, and I was elected to be sheriff here three times. And then there's all my work for the Church and the school board and the town council.'

Sarah smiled. 'Everybody knows what you've done to build Spanish Fork, Grandpa.' She paused and then asked, 'Do you mean there's something you haven't told us?'

My turn to smile.

'Well, I thought you might like to hear about my trip back to England in '83?'

Sarah's eyes lit up. 'Sure I would. 1883! Did you see the Queen? Did you go to London? What was it like? Is it true though?'

Full readable copy of this document on page 63

'Hold your horses, Sarah. I'll tell you all in my own time, so don't you go a flustering me!'

It was in April 1883, over forty years ago. There were 30 of us, all Elders of the Church and we had been chosen to go back to our home countries to do the Lord's work. The idea was the same as it is now that we went back to where we came from to research our family histories so that our dead relatives could be brought into the loving arms of the Church and be made members of God-fearing Mormon families even though they had passed away from this life. We hoped as well that we could find and convert new folk to our religion and take them back to Utah with us to build up our communities. Well, we set off to England in April, soon as the weather was reasonable, and travelled east to New York by the new railroad.

'What an experience that was, Sarah! Luxury ain't in it! We had a few stops and changed lines a few times and reached New York in five days. 2000 miles in five days! And sitting down all the way. Good Lord, when I think of the cruel time we had back in '54 when we crossed the Great Plains in ox – drawn wagons. And we lost people. Did I ever tell you about my friend Horace Howlett? Who died, and we had to bury him out there in an unmarked grave because of the Indians?'

'Yes Grandpa,' replied Sarah gently. 'Yes, you did and we remember him and all the others in our prayers.'

I nodded, remembering those distant times and wiped a tear from my eye, angry with myself for showing weakness: Horace was in a better world now and I would see him again soon enough.

'Well, let's get on with my tale.'

When we reached New York, we were told that we would have three days to look round the city before our ship sailed. And before you ask about that den of iniquity; that present day Sodom, Sarah, let me tell you now that I have never seen such a vision of Hell as I saw in that city! There was every sort of vice the Evil One has ever thought of. Some of us tried to meet with a few of the wretched creatures who lodged near our rooming house to show them a better life, but we were scorned and insulted in the vilest language. I was pleased to turn my back on that God forsaken place.

We crossed the Atlantic by steamship from New York to Liverpool, England. At first, I couldn't stop looking round that ship, remembering the old sailing ship we had crossed the Atlantic before. Everything was so smart and clean. But I'm sorry to say that I was not a good sailor and spent most of the journey in my bunk and wishing that the ship would stop rolling and pitching about: I was so ill, Sarah! And very thankful when we reached Liverpool after eleven days. From there we were sent to different parts of Britain: I went to Norwich, near to my birthplace in Crostwick, Norfolk.

'Why there, Grandpa?'

'Well, that was the place I'd known as a young man. That was how it worked: we were all sent to places where we might find old friends and relatives and start our work on familiar ground.'

The other men in the Mormon party elected me President of the Norwich group and we lost no time in getting down to work. I filled many notebooks collecting details of deceased members of the Jex family, covering many hundreds of miles on foot and by train. I distributed over 3000 pamphlets and spoke to hundreds of people and dozens of groups all over that part of England. I stayed with members of the Church and supported myself with my own money. I got a lot of names and dates from graveyards and sometimes local vicars would let me look at Church records – that was very productive, but most often the vicars would turn me away when they found out what I wanted the information for. I gathered details from talking to folks – older folks in particular - and from family Bibles, where families had noted down records of births, marriages and deaths which were so useful to me.

Most people I spoke to were interested when I told them about life in Utah and how productive the well managed farms were. I told them about the irrigation systems we had built up; about the new crops and the prosperity of the farmers. And, above all, I told them about the part the Mormon Church played in supporting the community both spiritually and physically. But it was hard sometimes to get uneducated farm labourers to realise what opportunities I was offering them and to persuade them that a better life by far was waiting for them. After all they were simple men and knew little more than muck and themselves; had never travelled more than a few miles from their birth places. But I would not be discouraged: I had been like them once, and look at me now! I saw it as a sacred duty to lift these men out of ignorance and false religion and bring them into the light of our faith.

Sometimes I failed badly. Like when I located a surviving close blood relative near my old home village, Crostwick. She was a single woman, my niece, being the daughter of my deceased sister Ann. I hadn't been in England very long and I guess I approached her all wrong. I must have seemed too boastful or somehow superior when I spoke to her in her humble cottage about the Mormon faith and the prosperity of the people. Anyhow, she listened me out and then, looking me straight in the eye, and said that she wanted nothing to do with me and my 'foolish notions and perverted faith'. She told me that she had heard tales of a Mormon missionary recruiting families with lots of female children so that men could take the girls as extra wives when they got them to America. She called him 'a stinking, slack-bellied old goat' and told me to go away and never visit her again.

'But most folk were polite, weren't they, Grandpa?' asked Sarah.

'Sure they were. English folk are friendly and I never had any more really bad encounters. My most successful contact was just before I left the Mission to Norfolk. I'd been there for about a year and was walking along a narrow street in Yarmouth when I noticed a sheet of torn and dirty paper blowing about at my feet. It was a handbill: the sort of advertising pamphlet that tradesman hand out. I was about to step over it when something made me look again and I was shocked to see the name 'JEX' printed on it. I picked it up, straightened it out, and saw that it was a handbill given out by a house painter and decorator in Yarmouth, name of Richard M. Jex! I firmly believe, Sarah, that the Lord's hand had guided me to that street and put me in contact with Richard.'

I'd never heard of him before and was hoping to learn about a new branch of our family. I walked to the address on the handbill and made myself known. I was received politely by Richard and his family. We quickly established that we were cousins and became firm friends from then on. Richard was the eldest son of Moses and Susan Jex. I was invited to stay with the family for a couple of weeks and spoke at length about my life and faith. I think that, being family, I was trusted to be telling the truth, particularly by Richard's two sisters, Ruth and Margaret. My newly found family and I spent many happy evenings, often talking far into the night about America and I rejoiced to see that my message was starting to take root. Ruth and Margaret decided to take the Faith and later returned with me to Utah. After a while, when the two girls had settled and had written to their parents, reassuring them that all was well, the rest of the family joined them in Spanish Fork: mother Susan was baptised in 1888, father Moses in 1889 and finally Richard and other family members made the journey to America and soon settled down into happy lives, most of them working in my timber and manufacturing businesses. They crossed the Atlantic in the USS Wisconsin in August 1890, Captain Leonard J. Jordan.

'So, Richard's sister, Ruth, must be the one who married your son, Richard Henry? That right, Grandpa?'

'That's right Sarah. She's been a good wife to Richard Henry. They had nine children, all well. Richard Henry was manager of the Cattleman's Bank in Salt Lake City. Went to Hawaii to do his stint as a missionary. But you know Sarah, my family is so large I could go rambling on for weeks, and I'm just too tired right now. Think I'll have a nap by the fire this afternoon.'

Moses Jex (William's cousins) and his
wife Susan Marie (formerly Smith).

Richard Henry Jex (William's son) and his wife, Ruth,
who was the daughter of Moses and Susan Marie
and was discovered by William on his missionary
visit back to Norfolk

The citizens engaged in the Diamond Creek encounter were: William Creer (in command), Albert Dimmock (killed), Warren E Davis, John H Koyle, William Jex, George Ainge, Alma C Davis, Llewellyn Jones, Wm J Thomas, Morgan Hughes, Joshua Brockbank, Leven Simmons, Ephraim Caffel, John Robertson, Adamson Shepherd (sent back to the settlement for help), and Jas. W Thomas, all of Spanish Fork.

William Jex died on April 5th, 1929.

Ihave ended William's story at this point as his family branches out into literally hundreds of separate people who have spread all over the US and further afield. For their details, including photographs, extending into the second, and third generations, please see "Jex Genealogy and Family History", Mary Jex Jolley (Moses Jex Genealogist,) circa 1950.

All the incidents in these accounts are true and have been well recorded in diaries, historical documents and newspaper articles, although I have created conversations in places where I could do so where it would be appropriate with the context. The character 'Sarah', to whom William speaks throughout this account, was first his niece and later his step daughter. To add to any confusion she referred to him, affectionately, as 'Grandpa'.

One major question remains: did William, during his missionary visit to Norfolk, meet my great grandfather Robert Jex, a letter carrier? William came to England in 1883 and I have a report of his attendance at the dedication of the Salt Lake City Temple in 1893. That leaves a possible span of ten years – plenty of time for him to have met Robert and his family. Left is the painting made by my grandfather in 1920 which he named The Letter Carrier.

Robert Jex was married to Lucy (nee Cable). They lived in Gorleston, in the cluster of Jex communities in that part of Norfolk and it is highly probable that William visited Robert during his mission. Robert and Lucy Jex had five children, the youngest being Albert Edward, who had been born in 1882.

Albert Edward Jex (below) grew up to become a skilled furniture maker and artist. He lived in Barton on Humber and was my maternal grandfather.

CERTIFICATE OF CITIZENSHIP.

United States of America, Territory of Utah, } ss

UTAH COUNTY.

PROBATE COURT FOR UTAH COUNTY.

Hon. .... Presiding.

Be it Remembered that on this 14th day of February A.D. 1866 William Jex a subject of Great Britain made application to become a citizen of the United States of America and produced to this Court satisfactory evidence that he on the 4th day of August A.D. 1844 in due form of law declared his intention to become such a citizen, and the Court being satisfied by the oaths of James Hilly Thomas & Thomas D Evans two citizens of the United States, that the said William Jex for one year last past has resided in this Territory, and for five years last past he has resided in the United States, during which time he has behaved as a man of good moral character: that he is attached to the principles of the Constitution of the United States, and well disposed to the good order of the inhabitants thereof, admitted him to be a citizen of the same: And Thereupon the said William Jex was sworn in due form of law to support the Constitution of the United States and absolutely and entirely renounce and abjure forever all allegiance and fidelity to every foreign prince, potentate, state and sovereignty whatever and particularly to Victoria Queen of Great Britain & Ireland whose subject he heretofore has been.

In Testimony Whereof, I hereunto set my hand and affix the Seal of said Court at my office in Provo this 14th day of February A.D. 1866 and of the Independence of the United States of America the Ninetieth.

................................, Pro. Clerk.

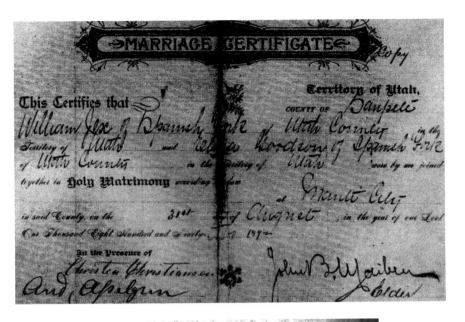